Webinar Profits Toolkit

AF894679

"If You've Ever Wanted to Create a Highly Profitable Webinar, But You Didn't Know Where to Start… Here's Your Solution!"

This collection of ten tools and resources will give you everything you need to impress your audience, fill your webinar seats, and generate loads of post-webinar sales…

… **And that's why I'm so pleased you now own it!**

Some time back I asked a client of mine how many webinars he's planning to run this year. He looked down. He shuffled his feet.

"None," he sheepishly replied.

"None?" I cocked an eyebrow.

"None," he confirmed.

I pressed him on this. I couldn't believe what he was telling me.

This is a guy whose business depends on him positioning himself as an authority in his niche. **He needed that connection.**

Sure, he was distributing eBooks, giving away free reports, doing guest blogging, had a decent presence across multiple social media channels and he was trying to get his name out in other ways.

But he wasn't doing webinars. And I knew it was going to kill his business sooner or later.

His competitors were doing webinars, and his clients were going to start taking notice.

Because you know what?

In today's social-media-driven business climate, trying to market your business without webinars is like trying to drive a car without wheels! Darn thing will make a lot of noise, but you won't get anywhere fast!

So this is what I told my client, and this is what I'm going to tell you too...

Savvy Marketers Everywhere Use Webinars!

Here Are 5 Rock Solid Reasons Why You Should Too...

1. Webinars are great lead-generation tools. People who are willing to spend 30-90 minutes of their time with you tend to be well-qualified prospects, which makes your webinar list very valuable!

2. Webinars are great for relationship-building. Whether you want to introduce yourself to a niche, establish yourself as an authority, or just develop better relationships with your market, a webinar is a great way to do it.

3. Webinars are great preselling tools. You get anywhere from 30 to 60 minutes to warm your audience up and put them in a buying state of mind... You can bet they'll hit the "buy now" button just as soon as the webinar is over!

4. Webinars enjoy a high perceived value. That means they're value much more than your run-of-the-mill eBook or free report, so people will pay more attention to your webinar than to just about any other type of information you can give them!

5. Holding a webinar is a fast way to create a product. You prep for your webinar, you spend 30-90 minutes delivering the content, and then you'll have a recording that you can sell or continue to distribute for months or years to come!

Point is, there are a lot of GREAT reasons to do webinars.

And I know one thing – you WANT to do them.

You wouldn't be reading this if you didn't want to start enjoying that big list and the profits you can generate from doing webinars.

And that's where I come in. I'm going to shortcut the learning curve and give you all the tools and resources you need to create webinars the fast, easy and profitable way!

These ten tools make light work of creating a webinar.

You'll get everything you need from help with creating your webinar scripts and slides, to marketing tips to fill your webinar seats!

End result?

A bigger list, more sales, and more revenue flowing through your business!

And if you're liking the sounds of those benefits, then let's get started...

Table of Contents

The 14-Day Guide to Creating Your Next Profitable Webinar

So you know you want to host a webinar, but you're not sure where to start? Use this 14-day planner to help you create your webinar.

Check it out...

Day 1: Pick Your Platform and Topic

Here are the things you need to do today:

- Pick your platform.
- Pick your topic and format.

Let's start with the platform. The bottom line here is that you want to choose one of the large, established and reputable platforms like GoToWebinar, WebinarPresenter, Zoom, or Webinar Jam.

> Avoid "no name" platforms that you're not familiar with, as your webinar could be a nightmare if you hit technical issues.

I personally use WebinarPresenter for pre-recorded webinars and Zoom for webinars up to 500 people. Over 500 attendees and I go with Webinar Jam.

So that's the easy part.

The next decision you need to make today is what you're going to talk about... To help you decide, ask yourself these questions:

- What product do you plan to promote on the backend?

- What topics are popular in your niche right now?

- What format will suit your needs the best for delivering your content and promoting the product?

NOTE: If you intend to have one or more guests join you, then today you'll also need to get in touch with them to see if they'll accept your invitation.

Day 2: Inform Your Marketing Partners

If you already have a list of joint venture partners who'll help you promote, then you need to alert them right away so that they can start planning when and how they'll promote.

Secondly, you'll want to prepare some marketing materials, which both you and your partners can use.

At a minimum, these materials include:

- A set of three to five emails to send out to your mailing lists. These should also work to post on a blog.

- Email "blurbs" that your partners can copy and paste into their regular newsletters.

- Social media blurbs.

Day 3: Create Your Lead Page

If you don't already have a domain name and hosting, you'll of course need to secure those first.

Specifically:

- You can get a domain using a registrar like NameCheap or Xerostar Domains
- You can get hosting through a company like BlueHost
- You may consider setting up the site using a free content management system such as WordPress.org.
- If you don't yet have an autoresponder, then secure an account through a reputable provider such as GetResponse or Mailerlite or any number of other established provider. I have moved from GetResponse to Mailerlite in the last year and have been very impressed.

Once that's all set up, then you need to create a lead page.

Day 4: Prep/Send Promotional Emails To Your List

Today you should put the final polish on the promotional emails that you and your marketing partners will send to your list. You can use the email templates included in this package to create them.

Once that's done, send off the first one today, and encourage your partners to do the same.

Day 5: Begin Other Promotional Methods

This may include:

- Posting on your social media platforms.
- Blogging about your webinar.
- Purchasing paid ads on platforms like Facebook.
- Doing guest blogging, with a byline that points to your webinar opt-in page.
- Asking your guests (if applicable) to help promote.

Day 6: Prepare Your Webinar Content

Now you need to start creating your content.

Depending on what you're doing, this may include:

- Drafting an outline for the points you want to cover during the webinar.
- Creating questions you'd like to ask your guests.
- Creating the text and graphics for slides (if you're doing a slide presentation video).
- Planning how to best demonstrate a product (where applicable).

In short: by the end of the day, you should have an outline of what you want to cover, along with preparing any supplemental content such as slides.

Day 7: Build Anticipation

Your webinar is just one week away, so today you'll want to do another round of promotions, including blogging, sending emails, posting on social media and so on.

In addition, you want to build anticipation and excitement with the people who've already registered for the webinar. So, send out an email reminding them of the date, time, and logon information, along with the benefits of attending.

Day 8: Create Bonus Handouts

This is optional, depending on what type of webinar you're creating. However, this is the day to create bonus materials that you'll hand out during or after the webinar.

Here are examples of the types of items you might offer as handouts:

- Outline of what topics you'll cover so that viewers can follow along. (And once the webinar is over, you may opt to transcribe it and send the transcriptions to attendees.)

- Supplemental bonus materials. For example, if your webinar is about driving traffic to and monetizing a blog, you may offer a handout that covers the prerequisite basics, such as the technical aspects of installing and customizing a blog.

- Resource/gear lists. This is a list of links and descriptions of any resources you mention during the webinar

- Tools to help people take action on what the just learned. This includes worksheets, checklists, templates, swipes, planners and more.

Day 9: Remind Marketing Partners

There are only five days left until your webinar, so you want to send your marketing partners a reminder to continue their promotional push. In addition, you'll want to give them additional content to help them promote.

> This might include anything from short promotional videos to graphic ads to social media blurbs.

As always, you'll use these same materials to help promote the event to your own contacts.

> **TIP:** Ask your marketing partners what they want and need to help them promote – and then create these materials and distribute them to all marketing partners.

Day 10: Continue With Promotions

Today you continue on with your own promotions. This includes the same list of promotions you did a few days ago, such as more blogging, posting on social media, purchasing ads and so on.

Here are a variety of short ads you can use to promote on social media, in signature lines and similar platforms and places:

Example 1

What if you could [get some amazing benefit] WITHOUT [dealing with bad consequences/side effects]? You'd be very interested, right?

Good news – now it's possible! Find out how here: [link to webinar opt-in page]

Example 2

On [day of the week] [time of the day, such as "evening"] you'll get the very rare opportunity to attend a webinar with guest expert [Name]. You'll [learn about some topic], plus [you'll get some other good benefit].

The best part is that it's all FREE! But there are only [number] seats left and they're going to go fast, so register now at [link to opt-in page].

Example 3

If you're like most [type of people], you're sick and tired of [trying to accomplish some goal but experiencing some undesired result instead].

Know this – it's not your fault! That's because [explain why it's not the reader's fault].

Now here's the good news…

You can [avoid this bad thing that is causing the unwanted results]. That's right, you can kiss [some bad result or other unwanted thing] goodbye for good! And best of all, you can learn exactly how to do it for FREE on [date and time] during the [name of webinar] webinar!

All you have to do is reserve your virtual seat now, and then prepare to [learn about some topic]. Click here to get started: [link] - and do it now before all the seats are gone!

Day 11: Proof And Polish Your Webinar Content

There are only three days left before your webinar, so you want to make sure all your materials are ready to go.

Check the following:

- Proof everything for accuracy.
- Check for spelling and grammatical errors on slides, handouts, and anything else your viewers will see.
- Be sure the content is useful and valuable all on its own.
- Check that your overall content naturally leads to the paid promotion at the end.
- Review your promotion to check that it identifies the problem, introduces your offer as the solution, gives your viewers solid reasons why they should buy this product, and provides a call to action.

- Ensure the content is engaging with novel information, relevant stories to emotionally engage people, a fast-pace, and a conversational tone.

Day 12: Do A Hard Promotional Push

There are just two days left until your webinar, so now you need to do one last (hard) promotional push and encourage your marketing partners to do the same.

You can naturally invoke urgency since the webinar is almost here and/or seats are filling up fast.

Here's an example blurb for social media or your blog...

The webinar you've been waiting for all year starts in just two days from now... and it's FREE! But hurry and reserve your seat now before they're all gone!

If you've ever wanted to [get some benefit] and [get some other benefit], then you're going to want to join this free event on [date and time]!

During this jam-packed hour you'll discover [main benefit], plus you'll even [learn some other little-known but valuable thing].

This webinar is 100% free, but it's only open to the next [number] people who reserve a seat now. So get yours by clicking here, because these last few seats are going to fill up fast!

NOTE: Be sure to send those who've already registered for your webinar a reminder that it's coming up in two days. As always, let them know the date and time, information about how to login, and remind them of the benefits to build excitement and boost attendance.

Day 13: Practice your delivery

Today you'll continue with your final promotional push and remind your partners to do the same. You can also send out a reminder to your attendee list to continue to build anticipation.

Today you'll also want to be sure you're ready to run your webinar.

This includes:

- Being sure that you're thoroughly familiar and comfortable with your chosen platform and all its features and functions.
- Practicing the delivery of your webinar. You may want to have a trusted friend critique you.
- Checking that all your supplemental materials are ready to go.

Day 14: Send out final reminders

Today is the day!

Here's what you need to do:

- Do one last promotional push to your contacts (if you have any seats left for the webinar).
- Send out a reminder to those who've registered to again provide all the essential information (such as time of the event and how to log in), as well as to build anticipation by sharing the benefits of the webinar.
- Get yourself psychologically ready for the webinar. You want to sound enthusiastic about your presentation, so do what you need to do to get "pumped up." Take a walk, listen to some upbeat music, talk to a friend, etc.
- Enjoy! You may feel nervous if this is your first webinar. Be prepared with a "Plan B" if something goes wrong, and don't stress about any perceived mistakes. Just go out, have fun, teach your participants something, and generate some revenue.

Once the webinar is over, you'll want to send out an email thanking people for attending, reminding them about the product you promoted, and to let them know when the replay will be up.

TIP: You'll also be sending out emails for the next several days after the webinar ends with the goal of generating post-webinar sales.

Reminder: There are templates for these specific emails included in this toolkit you'll get to them soon.

Okay Let's wrap things up...

Conclusion

Now that you have a planner in your hand, your next step is to put it to work for you. So go ahead and get started, because the sooner you do, the sooner you can reap the rewards of hosting a profitable webinar!

Creating The Perfect Product Pitch To Get A High Order Rate

One of the keys to having a successful webinar is to share a high-converting product pitch during the event that generates a lot of sales.

So how do you create this sort of perfect product pitch?

You can start with the following checklist guide, which takes you through these three steps:

- Step 1: Decide What Product to Promote
- Step 2: Design Your Webinar Around This Product
- Step 3: Deliver a Perfect Pitch

Take a look...

Step 1: Decide What Product to Promote

The first thing you need to do is pick a product to promote. This could be:

- Your own product. This of course is the best option, as this tends to be most profitable for you.

- An affiliate product. This is a good option if you don't yet have any of your own offers to promote, or if you're working with joint venture partners (especially during product launch, when interest is high).

- A product belonging to your guest expert. Depending on the terms of the joint venture that you set up with your guest expert, you'll probably use your affiliate link during the webinar to promote the product, so that you both make money from backend sales.

In all cases, you need to pick a product that has the following characteristics:

Characteristic #1: It's something your audience wants.

There's no use in promoting a product if there isn't a market that's eager and willing to pay money for it. That's why you'll want to do your market research to ensure you're promoting an in-demand product.

Now there are two ways to conduct this research, and your approach should include both:

1. Look at what people SAY they want. You can do this through surveys, through viewing their conversations online, by talking to them, etc.

2. Look at what people are actually buying. The best predictor of what people will buy tomorrow is to look at what they are actually buying today.

NOTE: Sometimes what people say they want and what they actually buy are two different things. That's why you should never use method #1 above in isolation. You can use it to confirm what you find out in #2, or even to gather a deeper insight about what your prospects want from a product. But don't use it a standalone market research method.

Here are the steps to take to determine what people want:

- Spend time "eavesdropping" and talking to your audience both online and offline. Online you can see what they're talking about on social media, on niche forums, on niche blogs and in similar communities. Offline you can learn more about them by attending niche events (trade shows, meetings, etc.).

- Survey your audience. Ask open-ended questions to get the best insights.

- See what your market is already buying. Visit marketplaces like Amazon.com, ClickBank.com, iTunes, JVZoo.com, and similar platforms to determine the bestsellers in your niche.

- Search for your niche keywords in Google. Then take note of what your competitors are selling. Also look at the paid (sponsored) ads both in Google as well as on your competitors' sites. If multiple people consistently pay money to advertise a particular type of product, that's a signal that there is a strong market for it.

- Search for your keywords in a keyword tool like WordTracker.com. This will give you an idea of what your market wants.

- Seek out trends on Google Trends. This will tell you if a particular topic is growing in popularity and/or holding stable over time, both of which are good things. (Beware of any topic that's declining in interest over time.)

Now here's the next characteristic to look for in a product you'd like to promote:

Characteristic #2: It's a profitable product for you to promote.

Generally, your own product is going to be the most profitable. If you're selling affiliate products, then make sure it's pricing and commission structure leaves you enough room to make a profit promoting the product.

> *TIP: Any product you promote is going to be more profitable for you if the sales letter is known to produce high conversions. Granted, your webinar is going to help presell prospects (which boosts conversions), but you'll still make more money if you're promoting a product with a persuasive sales letter.*

Characteristic #3: It's a high-quality product.

No matter how profitable or in-demand it is, don't promote it if it's not something that you would recommend to your best friend. Protect your buyers and your reputation by only promoting high-quality products.

> *TIP: In addition to reviewing the product, it's also a good idea to do your due diligence on the vendor if you're promoting an affiliate product. Be sure the vendor has an upstanding reputation in the niche before you attach your name to theirs (virtually forever) by promoting their product.*

Those are the main characteristics to look for when you're deciding what kind of product to promote. Once you select a quality, in-demand and profitable product, then you can move onto the next step...

Step 2: Design Your Webinar Around This Product

Now what you need to do is create a webinar that naturally leads to the promotion of your paid product. Your webinar content should be useful yet incomplete.

Let's break that down:

- Useful: Anyone who attends the webinar should have part of their problem solved. The webinar itself should standalone as a useful product. Your attendees should feel like it was well worth their time to attend (meaning they got a lot of value).

- ...yet incomplete: While the webinar solves part of a problem, it doesn't solve the entire problem. Your webinar naturally leads to the promotion of the paid product. Basically, anyone who likes your webinar will love the product you're promoting.

Here are a few examples of how to create a useful yet incomplete webinar that naturally leads to a paid product:

- Provide an overview of a process. The idea here is to give your viewers a step-by-step overview... but you save the in-depth details for a paid product. So your webinar tells people WHAT to do, but the viewers will need to purchase the paid offer to get the details of how to do it.

  For example, your webinar might give a step-by-step overview of how to start a business. Then during the webinar you'd sell a product that provides in-depth instruction, templates, checklists and more.

- Provide an in-depth treatment of *part* of a process. For this webinar you'd give your viewers the detailed instructions for completing one step of a process. Then you'd sell a product on the backend that teaches prospects how to complete one or more of the remaining steps.

For example, your webinar might show people how to set up and customize a WordPress blog. You'd then sell a guide on the backend that shows people how to create content and monetize the blog.

- Offer tips, tricks, and tools. Here you'd offer tips to help people solve their problems, and then sell an in-depth guide on the backend.

For example, your webinar might share five surefire tips for creating cash-pulling sales letters. You'd then sell a copywriting guide on the backend.

- Provide complete instruction on the frontend, sell tools on the backend. The idea here is to sell the tools to make it easier for people to complete the process they just learned about.

For example, your webinar might show dieters how to eat in a way that keeps them feeling satisfied while also boosting their metabolism. You'd then sell a meal-planning app on the backend.

So you get the idea – you want your webinar to pack in a lot of value for your viewers, yet it should be incomplete. That way, the webinar naturally leads to your product pitch.

Now before we get to the product pitch, let me share with you one more tip...

Try to create a webinar that people will **refer to repeatedly**.

The more often someone refers back to your webinar, the more they'll see your links and calls to action.

So, what sort of webinar are people likely to refer to often?

Check out these ideas:

- In-depth information. If you pack your webinar full of really good information, then people are going to watch it more than once just to be sure they haven't missed anything.

- New information. If you can provide tips, tricks, and strategies that no one else is sharing, then your viewers will refer back to your webinar to remind themselves of those novel tips and tricks.

- Bonus tools. You may wish to provide text-based tools to go along with your webinar. These include items that help people take action, such as checklists, worksheets, templates and more. Your webinar can provide instruction for making the most of these tools, and the tools themselves can include your links and calls to action.

And now the last step...

Step 3: Deliver a Perfect Pitch

So, at this point you've selected an in-demand product to promote, AND you've created your webinar around this product (so that you can naturally promote the product during the webinar). At some point during the webinar, often at the end, you'll deliver your pitch.

Use this mini-checklist to help you create that high-converting pitch...

<u>Identify The Problem</u>

You accomplish this in two steps:

- Note the signs and symptoms of the problem so that viewers realize they have that problem. E.G., "Do you lose the weight on a diet, only to gain it all back again?"

- Remind viewers of the pain of their problem. "It's humiliating when you take your shirt off at the beach and people snicker at your love handles."

<u>Introduce the Solution</u>

Now you introduce hope to your prospects by introducing your product and giving a quick summary of what it will do for them...

E.G.,

"Now here's the good news - you can start feeling GOOD on the beach again. You can have jaws-dropping when they see your washboard abs. And it all begins with [insert name of product]..."

<u>Inform Viewers Of The Benefits</u>

Once you've given prospects and overview of the product, now you get down to specifics by sharing the biggest five or ten benefits of the product.

> NOTE: Since this is a webinar, whenever possible you should show your prospects the product as you introduce it and share its benefits. If it's a digital information product or software, then you can share your desktop

as you go through the table of contents or dashboard. For physical products, you can do a demo of how they work while you talk about it.

Let's continue with the weight-loss product example.

Here is an example of a benefit statement where you tell viewers what the product will do for them while arousing curiosity in the process:

"You'll discover which common food you should NEVER eat when you're trying to lose weight! Hint: You've probably eaten it in the last 72 hours, and it's wreaking havoc with your metabolism!"

Inspire Action

Once you have people excited about the product and you've built up the value, then you create a call to action.

This is where you tell them what to do and why.

For example:

"I'm dropping a link below in the text box, and I urge you to click on it right now and then review the page just as soon as we end this call. Simply put - if you're looking to get great results, then you're going to want to get your hands on this product. So click that link right away to get started…"

Conclusion

There you have it – a step-by-step process for delivering the perfect product pitch during your webinar.

It starts with picking a good product, designing the webinar around the product, and then delivering a compelling pitch.

NOTE: Be sure to also follow up with your webinar viewers by email to remind them of the reasons to buy the product. You can further boost conversions by offering a limited-time discount.

The <u>10</u> Most Important Parts Of Your Webinar And How To Make Them Awesome

You're getting ready to host a webinar, and you want to makes sure it all goes off without a hitch, you get a lot of attendees, and you generate a lot of sales on the backend.

Use this 10-point checklist to make sure you have all the essential ingredients place.

Take a look...

1. The Webinar Platform

A lot of people get all wrapped up in the content of their webinar and give very little thought to what webinar platform they'll use to deliver this content. Next thing you know, the platform crashes – and the webinar needs to be postponed.

Tell you what, that <u>does not</u> make a very good impression!

Point is, you need a webinar platform that you can depend on. That's why you'll want to go with the platform that I've already sung the praises of like WebinarPresenter and Zoom and avoid the small service offerings and overpriced clunky ones.

Don't be swayed by low prices, plugins or budget offerings as a good deal becomes a horrible deal when you run into technical difficulties during your webinar.

The second thing you need to do to make sure your webinar is awesome is to practice on the platform BEFORE you give your webinar. You want to be perfectly comfortable and familiar with all the platforms controls and functions, so that you can do things like field questions, mute and unmute yourself and your guests, share your desktop and more.

2. The Opt-In Page

If you want to get a lot of attendees, then you need a persuasive opt-in page. Check that yours includes the following ingredients:

- Professional design. You want to make a good impression, and that means starting with a good-looking opt-in page. Personally, I cannot speak highly enough about Kickpages to use when building great looking pages fast. I have tried them all, and still own several but I use Kickpages exclusively at this point.

- An attention-getting, benefit-driven headline. You want to put your biggest benefit front and center. E.G., "Free Webinar Shows You How to Save $375 On Your Home Heating and Cooling Bills!"

- A list of the top benefits of the webinar. E.G., "You'll discover a simple trick that takes just five minutes to complete, but it could double your sales letter conversion rate!"

- A call to action. This is where you specifically tell people to reserve their seat. E.G., "Fill out the form below now to reserve your seat – and hurry before they're all gone!"

Need help with this part? Check the opt-in page templates included later in this manual.

3. The Pre-Webinar Emails

If your landing page did a good job, then you're going to get plenty of sign-ups for your webinar. But that doesn't mean you'll actually have a lot of people watching the webinar. That's why you'll want to send out a series of emails that gets people excited about the upcoming webinar.

Check that your emails include these ingredients:

- An enticing subject line. You need to get people to open the emails in order for these emails to be effective. E.G., "In just two days your dieting problems will be over!"

- The benefits of the webinar. The idea here is to get people excited so that they'll attend. E.G., "You'll find out what you can eat right now that will give your metabolism a huge boost!"

- A reminder of when the webinar will happen and how people can attend. Don't assume people know this information. In every email you send, you should remind people of the date and time (including the time zone), along with the information they need to get on the call.

This information may include:

- A link to the webinar platform.
- Instructions about passwords (if applicable).
- What sort of hardware and software they need to participate?

If you need help with this step, check the email templates included in this package. You can swipe them, modify them to fit your needs, and blast them out to get your audience excited and get them on the webinar.

4. The Title Of Your Webinar

A lot of people are going to decide whether to attend your webinar based on the title of it, so make sure it's awesome. That means creating a benefit-driven title.

Check out these five templates:

- The #1 Way To [Get a Benefit]. E.G., "The #1 Way To Get Rid of Cellulite."
- The Quick and Easy Way to [Get a Benefit]. E.G., "The Quick and Easy Way to Sell Your Home For Top Dollar."
- The Insider Secrets of [Getting a Benefit]. E.G., "The Insider Secrets of Crafting Million-Dollar Sales Letters."
- [Number] Surefire Tips and Tricks for [Getting a Benefit]. E.G., "Seven Surefire Tips and Tricks For Writing a Bestselling Romance Novel."
- A Simple [Number]-Step System For [Getting a Benefit]. E.G., "A Simple Three-Step Process For Getting All The Business Funding You Need."

Those are just a few ideas to get you started.

5. The Guest Experts (Where Applicable)

If you plan on having anyone else on the webinar as an expert or interviewee, then be sure you do your due diligence before extending an invitation.

That's because this person is going to be "linked" to you indefinitely. So you want to make sure your guests have upstanding and long-established reputations in your niche and beyond.

> TIP: You can do most of your research with a Google search. Simply search for the person's name, business name, website, and even the name of their products. Beware of anyone who has a pattern of complaints lodged by customers, affiliates, suppliers, or business partners.

6. The Content Of Your Webinar

You can whip people into a frenzy and get them flooding your webinar... but they'll hang up just as quick if your content doesn't hold their interest.

Check out these points as you're planning the content for your webinar:

- Be sure the content is something people WANT. Do your market research to determine if your chosen topic is something people are interested in.
- Deliver what you promised. Be sure your sales/opt-in page matches up with the actual content you're delivering.

- Create high-quality slides. If you're doing a slide-presentation, then be sure to have professional graphics and nicely formatted slides to hold attention.

- Change the visuals. Whether you're doing a slide-presentation webinar, a demo, or a talking head webinar, it's a good idea to change the visuals to keep people interested. For example, if you're doing a talking head webinar, then you might demonstrate how to do something (rather than just talking at the camera). This makes the webinar more appealing, engaging, and useful.

- Create an outline, but don't overly script your delivery. That's because you don't want to sound like a robot when you do your webinar. Your outline will keep you track without you reading every word of a script.

- Practice your delivery. Be sure you're speaking in a friendly, conversational tone.

- Engage your audience.

  This includes:

  - Telling stories to emotionally engage the audience.
  - Asking them thought-provoking questions.
  - Fielding questions from the audience (directly engaging with them).
  - Staying focused on their problems and how to fix those problems.

Also, be sure the content of your webinar naturally leads to the product you're pitching.

Which brings us to the next piece...

7. The Product You're Promoting

One of the jobs of your webinar is to build a responsive list. Another of its jobs is to help you generate post-webinar sales.

That's why you need to make sure you're promoting a product with these characteristics:

- It's something your prospects really want. (Hint: do your market research to find out what they're already buying.)

- The product is directly related to the content of the webinar.
- It's a high-quality product that you're proud to promote.

8. The Product Pitch

The second part of generating sales is to create a good pitch at the end of your webinar.

This includes:

- Stirring up the pain of the problem. You want to remind people of how unhappy they are with this problem, and how frustrating it's been to try to solve the problem.
- Getting people to imagine the joy of the solution. Now you introduce your offer as the solution to their problems. This gives people hope. It makes them feel better, especially if you can get them imagining they'll have good results.
- Sharing the benefits of the product. Here's where you list all the reasons why your viewers should buy the product. Basically, this is the answer to the questions, "Why should I buy this product, and what will it do for me?"
- Offering proof. People are naturally going to be a little skeptical of your claims. That's why it's a good idea to offer proof, such as information from a case study. Whenever possible, produce "live" proof during the webinar.

  For example, if you're claiming an advertising strategy has produced great results for you, then log into our traffic logs and PayPal account while you're on the air to show proof.

- Providing a call to action. Finally, you need to end this pitch by specifically telling people what you want to do next.

  E.G.,
  `"Go to www.milesaustin.com/brand/right now to pick up this amazing course and templates!"`

9. The Pace Of Your Webinar

One of the reasons people get bored during a webinar is because the pacing is too slow.

Here are factors that can slow down your webinar:

- You're talking too slow. A slow rate of speech and a monotone voice oozes boredom. Show your enthusiasm by talking more quickly and changing the tone of your voice.

- You're talking about personal things too much. It's okay to touch on a personal note to build credibility or to tell a relevant story. But if you talk about yourself too much (rather than focusing on the audience's problems), eventually your viewers are going to start thinking, "Who cares?"

- You're interacting on a personal level with the audience too much. Interacting is a good thing, such as when you field questions from an audience. But if you're just doing small talk with one person, the rest of your audience is going to get bored (especially those who watch the replay later).

- You're not changing the visuals enough. This is particularly true if you're doing a slide-presentation. If you sit on one slide for too long, the audience is going to get bored.

TIP: Practice your webinar ahead of time and ask a trusted friend to critique your delivery.

10. The Post-Webinar Emails

Once the webinar is over, you want to keep the excitement going and start generating sales by sending a series of post-webinar emails.

Check that your emails include these points:

- An enticing subject line. Again, use benefit-driven or curiosity-arousing subjects to get people to open your emails.

- A recap of the main points and benefits of the webinar. You'll want to encourage people to watch it again (or watch it for the first time if they didn't attend the live event).

- The benefits of the product you're promoting. Remind people of the biggest reasons they should get their hands on this product.

- A call to action. This is where you specifically instruct people to order the product now. For best results, stir up a sense of urgency. One good way to do this is with a limited-time discount.

  E.G.,

  "Order in the next 72 hours, and you'll enjoy a whopping 50% discount! Click here to claim your discount right now…"

Conclusion

As you can see, there are a lot of pieces and parts you need to snap together in order to have a winning webinar. This checklist stepped you through the top ten pieces.

If you apply what you just learned above, you'll enjoy plenty of attendees at your webinars, a big mailing list, and nice stream of post-webinar sales!

15 Content Recipes That Will Impress Attendees

If you've been planning your webinar, then you've probably been thinking about how to approach your webinar.

Most people think about two or three different ways to do it, which is pretty limiting. That's why you're about to discover 15 content recipes that will keep your attendees engaged, impressed, and staying on your webinar right to the very end.

> TIP: These different recipes may be presented in different recipes. For example, a "how to" video might be presented as a talking head video, a demo video, or even a slide presentation. Pick your content recipe first, and then decide the best format for its presentation.

Check them out...

1. The Step-By-Step "How To" Webinar

This is a popular format because viewers tend to find it quite useful. Basically, you teach them how to complete a specific task or achieve a goal.

For example, you might give people the step-by-step process for setting up a blog, restoring the interior of a classic car, or selling a home.

The outline for this webinar would look like this:

A. Introduction, where you build anticipation.

B. The meat of the webinar, where you share the steps of each process.

C. A product pitch, where you share a tool or resource to make the process easier.

D. The conclusion, where you recap the content and provide a call to action to buy the item.

Next...

2. The Tips and Tricks Webinar

Here's where you offer tips to make it easier for people to achieve a goal.

E.G., "Ten Tips for Getting Top Dollar When You Sell Your Home."

Here's one way to structure the webinar:

A. Introduction.

B. The meat of the content, where you share your tips.

C. Here you'll share a tip which will involve using a certain product to achieve a goal. For example, if a tip for bodybuilders is to consume one gram of protein per pound every day, then you might promote a specific brand of whey protein to make it easier to implement the tip.

D. Conclusion, where you emphasize the benefits of the product and provide a call to action.

3. The Tools Webinar

Here's where you present tools to make a process easier. This might be a gear list, a list of software, or even specific non-tangible tools people can put to work for them (such as a calming breathing exercise to help reduce stress).

E.G., "The Top 10 Tools Every Online Marketer Ought To Be Using."

The beauty of this webinar is that you can promote multiple products from within the same webinar.

Here's an example outline:

A. Introduction – go over the ways that the following tools help people complete a task faster, easier and/or better.

B. List your tools, along with specific reasons why you use those exact tools. If possible, demonstrate each of these tools live during the webinar.

C. Conclusion. Go over the reasons again why people should use the tools and encourage them to start using these tools too.

TIP: You'll want to provide a text-based copy of your list of tools – such as a downloadable PDF with links – so that your viewers have all the links at their fingertips.

4. The Mistakes Webinar

During this webinar you'd share the most common mistakes people make in the niche and how to avoid them.

E.G., "The Top Five Fat-Loss Mistakes You're Making Right Now!"

Here's a sample outline:

A. Introduction, where you build fear about making these particular mistakes.

B. The meat of the webinar, where you share the top mistakes and how to avoid them.

C. How a specific product can help people either:

    1) Avoid making other mistakes. Here you might promote an information product that shortcuts the learning curve.

    2) Avoid making a specific mistake. For example, you might recommend that marathon runners buy a specific pair of shoes (through your affiliate link) to help ward off common problems such as blisters.

D. Conclusion, where you reiterate the danger of making these mistakes, and call people to action to purchase the product to protect themselves.

5. The "Ways To" Webinar

Here's where you present different ways to accomplish a goal or complete a task. E.G., "Five Ways To Shave Strokes Off Your Golf Game."

Here's an example outline:

A. Introduction, where you whet people's appetite for what's to come by sharing benefits and arousing curiosity. E.G., "You're about to discover the absolute easiest way to boost your conversion rates."

B. The meat of your webinar, where you share your "ways." If the ways can't be used together to achieve a goal, then you should provide the pros and cons of each method. For example, one way to lose weight is with a moderate carb diet, and another way is with a low carb diet. But these ways can't be used together.

C. Here you share one of the ways, tout its benefits, and then promote a related product or service. For example, if your webinar talks about different ways to set up an ecommerce store, you might promote the Shopify platform.

D. Conclusion. Here you recap the main points of the webinar, and then end with a call to action where you promote the product or service.

6. The Interview Webinar

As the name implies, this is where you bring a guest onto the webinar. You might interview the guest, or the guest might interview you.

Here's an example outline:

A. Introduce the guest. Build credibility, and basically let viewers know why they should listen to this person.

B. Interview the guest to uncover good tips and strategies for the niche. Example questions:

    What mistakes did you make when you were just starting out?
    If you were starting in the niche today, what would you do first?
    What is the best way to [get some benefit]?

C. Conclusion: Thank the guest, and then promote the guest's product at the end of the webinar.

NOTE: While you'll want to draw up the questions ahead of time, and you may even give your guest an idea of the sorts of questions you'll ask, do NOT script the interview. If both of you are just reading your questions and answers, the interview will sound stilted and even fake.

7. The Guest Panel Webinar

This is where your webinar includes two or more experts to create a "panel" to discuss a specific topic.

E.G., "What Do Top Personal Trainers Really Think About Low-Carb Dieting?"

This webinar will be most engaging if you can bring on different types of experts who will have differing opinions about how best to achieve a goal.

For example, you might bring on a dietician, personal trainer, body builder and health professional to talk about the best way to lose weight.

You won't create an outline, per se.

But here's how you might structure this webinar:

A. Introduction. Here you'll introduce each person on your panel and build their credibility.

B. Ask a question, and a select one panelist to answer. Then give each panelist an opportunity to answer. If two panelists disagree, you may spend extra time letting them "argue" their case (makes for great content).

C. You'll want to prepare a few questions ahead of time to keep the conversation moving along, but generally a panel will tend to take on a life of its own.

D. Conclusion. Thank your panelists for their time. As you thank them individually, you can promote their products or services.

Note: Since you may be promoting several offers, it's a good idea to provide a PDF of the offers mentioned during the call.

8. The Product Review Webinar

This is where you review a product, including both its pros and cons, and then make a recommendation at the end (assuming you like the product, you'll recommend it).

Here's an outline for this webinar:

A. Introduction—what the product is and what it does.

B. Demo the product whenever possible.

C. Go through the features of the product, highlighting the benefits.

D. Highlight the potential weaknesses of the product. Whenever possible, handle these objections (i.e., let people know why these weaknesses aren't deal-breakers).

E. Offer your recommendation, and let people know who would most benefit from using the product. Then offer a call to action to purchase the product.

9. The Case Study Webinar

This type of webinar helps sell a product by providing proof that the product works.

Here's an example outline:

A. Introduction of the product and what it does.

B. Introduction of the person who did the case study. (Ideally, this should be someone just like your viewers, so that they realize they can get similar results.)

C. "Before" / baseline data. For example, if it's a weight loss case study, you'd share before pics as well as weights and measurements.

D. Data after starting to use the product. This may be data reported hourly, daily, weekly, or monthly, depending on what the process is. For example, with a weight loss case study you might present weekly measurements, pics, and other proof.

E. Conclusion – talk about how well the product worked to get the desired results. Show proof. Encourage viewers to purchase the product and start using it for themselves.

10. The "Live Proof" Webinar

This is another proof video, except here you provide "live" proof.

For example, if you're selling a guide on how to build a responsive list, you might send out an email to your list live on the air and watch the sales pour in.

There is no outline here, as this is a bit unpredictable.

Basically:

- Let people know what you're going to do and what you expect to happen.
- Provide your live proof.
- Recap the results and encourage people to buy the related offer.

11. The Group-Coaching Webinar

Here's where you field questions from the audience and answer them during the broadcast. For best results, you might solicit questions ahead of time so that you can prepare thorough answers and give the most useful responses.

Naturally, the outline here is just the basic question and answer format.

You'll want to answer one or more of the questions by providing a product recommendation. Or you can let your expertise speak for itself, and then promote your information product at the end.

12. The Training Webinar

The idea behind this webinar is to show viewers how to do something. In particular, you might show them the best way to use a particular tool (and then you promote that tool from within the webinar).

For example, you might train viewers how to segment a mailing list using Mailerlite, which lets you naturally promote the service at the end of the webinar.

So the outline is your basic structure like this:

A. Introduction (whet appetite for what is coming).
B. Step-by-step training and instruction.
C. Conclusion where you promote the tool or other product.

13. The Fear-Logic-Gain Webinar

This is a direct-sales webinar, where you touch on different factors (fear, logic and gain) that will appeal to different segments of your audience.

Here are the parts of this webinar:

A. Introduction, where you introduce the product.

B. Gain: where you share the benefits of the product.

C. Logic: where you provide rational reasons to buy the product (backed by data or science).

D. Fear: where you give prospects a reason to buy now, such as fear of missing out on a great deal.

E. Conclusion: provide a call to action, where you promote the product.

14. The VSL-Style Webinar

This is a video-sales-letter (VSL) style webinar, where you structure your webinar in the same format as a sales letter.

Here's a sample outline:

A. Identify the problem.

B. Remind people of the pain of this problem.

C. Introduce a product as the solution to this problem.

D. Share the benefits of this solution.

E. Offer proof (and demo the product where possible).

F. Handle objections.

G. Justify the price.

H. Call prospects to action by encouraging them to buy the product.

15. Behind the Scenes Webinar

This is where you take your viewers behind the scenes. You might take them live to an event (like a trade show), or you can just give them a behind-the-scenes look at your niche. For example, a personal trainer might show what all goes into planning a fitness boot camp.

Conclusion

As you can see, there are plenty of content recipes you can use to engage, impress, and inspire action in your viewers. What you choose depends on what you're teaching and what you're promoting.

But the bottom line is, don't just limit yourself to one or two webinar styles, when there are so many different kinds to suit your needs.

50 Ways To Promote Your Webinars And Fill Every Seat

You've got a great idea for an awesome webinar. You just know your attendees will love it. But what you need to do next is fill those seats.

How do you do it?

By employing the following 50 surefire ways for filling up webinar seats. Take a look...

1. Blog about it.

But don't just make one post – create a series where you build anticipation for the event and encourage people to reserve a seat before they're all gone.

2. Do guest blogging.

You can create articles related to the event and distribute them as guest articles. Be sure to include a link to the webinar opt-in page inside your byline (and/or directly within the article, if allowed).

3. Join relevant discussions on other blogs.

For example: if you're holding a webinar on low-carb dieting, then join discussions on other blogs on this same topic. Where allowed, drop a link to your webinar registration page as your signature link.

4. Tell your social media contacts.

Tweet about it. Post on your Facebook timeline. Share on Google+. Post a related image on Instagram. And in all cases, use relevant hashtags to bring in more traffic.

5. Join discussions on social media.

In other words, post on other peoples' social media pages, and link to your webinar opt-in page (where allowed).

6. Email your list (repeatedly).

Just as you should create a series for your blog to boost conversions, so too should you create a series of emails to send out to your list.

7. Design a promotional video.

This can be a "sneak peek" video where you tease some of the webinar content, or it can be directly promotional (like a video sales letter). Or you can do both! Then post your videos on YouTube, on your blog, and across social media.

8. Send out a press release.

You can send your press release to local media, as well as distribute it to a wider audience using a service like PRWeb.com.

9. Use a notification bar.

These are also called "attention bars" or even "hello bars." The point is to overlay these attention-getting bars on the high-traffic pages of your site, which will call special attention to your webinar.

> TIP: You can use a tool like ConvertBox to create these bars (no coding knowledge required).

10. Post an ad in your blog's sidebar.

This could be either a text or graphical ad. You may even use an ad rotator to display several different ads for your webinar.

11. Create a "featured post" on your blog.

Draw special attention to your event by "pinning" a post at the top of your blog or using that post as the front page of your blog. When possible, embed your opt-in form directly into the page.

12. Post a "pinned post" on social media.

Same as above, but this time you feature your upcoming webinar on social media, such as on your Facebook Page timeline.

13. Ask your JV partners to promote.

If you currently have joint venture partners, you can ask them to help you promote your event. If you don't yet have JV partners, it's time to start developing relationships in your niche.

TIP: If you don't have JV Partners or affiliates then you should check out the incredible Partner Traffic Blueprint

14. Consider an affiliate program.

The idea is to have affiliates promote the free webinar on the front end, and they'll use their affiliate links to get credit for any sales on the backend. The folks at Thrivecart offer the very best affiliate software I have found and count on it every day in my business.

15. Create viral content for social media.

For example, create a useful infographic that's highly related to your webinar, and then post your webinar link at the bottom of it. Encourage your networks to share it widely.

16. Buy advertising on niche sites.

You might even ask your colleagues if they'd be willing to sell you a prime advertising spot on their websites, such as on their blog.

17. Purchase solo advertising.

If you know niche newsletters who accept advertising, then purchase a small ad or even a solo ad. It's a good idea to do a small ad buy first, and then purchase more advertising if the first ad goes well.

18. Use Facebook's ad platform.

For best results, just be sure to use the ad editor to focus in on as narrow of a target market as possible.

19. Consider using Google AdWords.

Again, use highly targeted keywords to attract the right audience. You'll also want to test and track your ads to optimize conversions.

20. Test advertising on sites like Reddit.

You can buy ads for relatively inexpensively on Reddit. Be sure to choose a targeted sub-Reddit on which to place your ad.

21. Advertise using a third-party service.

The idea here is to test out an ad broker such as BlogAds.com, which will place your ads on targeted websites.

22. Swap ads with other marketers.

You can swap email ads, social media ads, blog ads or even thank you-page ads.

23. Use signature lines on niche forums/communities.

Participate in group discussions in Facebook Groups and across forums and use your signature line to advertise your webinar opt-in page.

24. Place local ads.

You can place them in local newspapers or even on local websites. You might also consider placing them on local radio.

25. Use "guerilla marketing" methods locally.

For example, pass out flyers at a local related tradeshow or expo.

26. Do local Joint Ventures with related businesses.

For example, you might arrange to insert flyers into customers' shopping bags in niche stores, in exchange for advertising your partner's business.

27. Create a viral contest to raise awareness.

You can even give everyone who shares the webinar opt-in page an extra entry into your contest.

28. Capture exit traffic.

If you have traffic coming into your blog or other web pages that isn't joining your list for other reasons, then you'll want to put one more offer in front of them – an invitation to join your webinar.

> TIP: No tech experience? No problem. You can use the ConvertBox app to redirect exiting traffic to your webinar opt-in page.

29. Put an ad on your own thank you/download pages.

This includes the thank you pages for those signing up for your other free offers, as well as the payment confirmation pages for customers.

30. Announce your webinar on listing sites.

Two popular sites include www.webinarbase.com and www.tellonline.org. You can find others by searching Google.

31. Create an event on Facebook for your webinar.

Be sure to invite all your contacts to this event and encourage them to join. In turn, this has a bit of a viral and social proof effect, as people take note that their friends are joining your webinar.

32. Craft a promotional slideshow.

This can be a sneak peek of your webinar with some teaser content. You can then post this slideshow on www.slideshare.com.

33. Offer an incentive for attendees to tell their friends.

For example, give people who've already registered the chance to get a free related eBook, app, video or other bonus in exchange for sharing information about your webinar with their friends.

34. Announce an upcoming webinar within your current webinar.

This is a great tactic to use if you tend to put on a lot of regular webinars, as you can mention your upcoming webinars (or send them to a generic "upcoming webinars" page to see what's coming next).

35. Post an original article on LinkedIn.

This works well if you're giving webinars to business owners or other professional people. Be sure your article is directly related to the content of your webinar, so that anyone who is interested in the article will want to join the webinar.

36. Do a sneak peek on social media.

For example, do a Facebook Live video for 10 or 15 minutes, where you share some tips and tease the upcoming webinar content. Then promote your webinar at the end.

37. Find influencers to share the news.

There are people in your niche who may not necessarily be marketers, but they tend to have a lot of influence in the niche. Find these people, befriend them, give them sneak peeks at your content, and ask them to spread the word about your webinar.

38. Post local event listings.

You can post these on local websites, local pages on Facebook, and even in local newspapers.

39. Give interviews.

Make yourself available for both text and multimedia interviews with local media, talk radio, and other experts in your niche.

40. Design a webinar series. << (one of my favorites)

One good way to fill your seats is by putting on a series, such as "Three Secrets Everybody Ought to Know About Retiring Early" (with each of the three secrets revealed in three separate webinars). The beauty is that with each webinar, excitement will grow, and more people will hear about the event, which in turn will fill your seats.

41. Change your social media images.

A good way to draw attention to your webinar on social media (other than posting), is to change your profile photos and/or cover pics to graphical ads for your webinar.

42. Create a contest for marketing partners.

Earlier you learned about how to create a contest for your prospects to drum up attention. Another way to fill up seats is to create a contest for your marketing partners. You might offer cash rewards, gift cards or other valuable prizes to those who refer the biggest number of attendees.

43. Place an announcement on your homepage.

The homepage of your website (or websites) is prime real estate – so put an announcement for your webinar front and center, right at the top of the page.

44. Hang flyers locally.

You should focus on hanging them in places where your target market is likely to see them. For example, if you're doing a dog training webinar, then hang them at pet supplies stores (with permission).

You can also hang them in other high-traffic areas like restaurants and grocery stores. It's not as targeted, but it's a quick, easy and cheap way to get more people seeing your webinar advertisement.

45. Insert ads in your membership sites.

Whether they are free or paid membership sites, you can put an ad front and center in your member dashboard. In other words, make sure the webinar announcement is the first thing members see when they log in. (As always, be sure to email your members as well.)

46. Place ads in existing eBooks and similar products.

This tactic works particularly well if you do regular webinars, as you can send customers to a general webinar page that lists all upcoming webinars. In other words your promotion stays evergreen as long as you keep doing webinars.

47. Insert ads into your existing lead magnets.

Same as above, except you can insert the promotion into your lead magnets. This includes videos, eBooks, apps and other lead magnets. Again, send leads to a general "upcoming webinar" page so that your promotion stays evergreen.

48. Use search engine optimization.

This is another tactic to use if you do regular webinars, as you can optimize an evergreen "upcoming webinars" page to draw traffic from the search engines.

For example, if you do weight loss webinars, then you might optimize for words such as "weight loss webinar," "dieting webinar," "fat loss webinar," "free dieting information" and similar. (Naturally, check your keyword tool to determine which words to use.)

49. Encourage attendees to spread the word.

In this case, you're not even offering an incentive. Instead, simply ask your attendees to tell their friends.

E.G., "Know someone else who'd love to attend? Click here to tell them about the webinar – they'll thank you for it!"

50. Ask your guests to spread the word.

Whether you have a single guest expert or an entire panel, ask them to help you promote the webinar. You can even incentivize this proposal, such as by giving them a cut of backend sales.

Conclusion

There you have it – 50 ways to promote your webinar!

Now there's just one thing to do... put these surefire methods to work for you!

Your Fill-In-The-Blanks Webinar Template...

One of the most popular types of webinars is the training webinar, where you teach your viewers how to complete some specific process or achieve a goal.

Now if you've never done one before, you might be scratching your head and wondering how to go about it.

Wonder no more – below you'll find a complete fill-in-the-blank template you can use to create your webinar script.

Here you go...

Webinar Script Template

<Get on the webinar early and spend some time greeting people and talking to them as they arrive on the call. Ask them where they're from and other small talk. Engaging in small talk will make you feel less nervous, plus it builds a relationship with attendees. This makes it more likely they will 1) Stay for the entire call, 2) Ask questions or otherwise participate and 3) Buy what you're selling.>

Looks like it's time to get started!

First off, I'd like to thank you all for attending the [Name of Webinar] webinar. My name is [Your Name], and I'll be your host for the [evening/afternoon/event/etc.].

Now if you're not familiar with me, then allow me to take a few moments to introduce myself. I've been <working in some field> for <some length of time now. E.G., "11 years."] And during that time, I've learned a whole lot about [some very specific topic that's relevant to this webinar].

Let me be clear here - this isn't a case of me just reading about [topic] and learning about it that way. I've been in the trenches every day, testing out <type of> ideas, and have used my strategies to great success for both myself and my clients.

For example, [insert a specific example of how your strategies have achieve some very specific result - the idea here is to build credibility with your audience.]

So that gives you a little bit of background on me. Now let's jump into [today's/tonight's/this morning's/etc.] topic, which is [insert the topic]…

What you're going to learn over about the next [number of minutes or hours, e.g., "… over the next hour"] is how to [get some specific result]. Specifically:

- You're going to discover a super-slick way to [get some benefit].
- You'll find out [what tools or resources to use to get these benefits].
- Plus you'll discover the top [number] mistakes and how to avoid them.

So let's get started…

Now if you've been wanting to [get some benefit], then you know that one of the biggest problems you face is [describe the problem]. What you're going to like about the following process is that it [explain how it virtually eliminates the common problem].

So the first thing you need to do is [explain briefly what this step entails].

Now if you're like a lot of people, you're going to be tempted to [do the process in some certain way]. But if you do that, [you'll end up with some undesired result]. And that's a big mistake, right? It's going to [create some undesired effect… cost time, cost money, etc.].

So what you want to do instead is [explain the right way to approach the problem, step-by-step]. What this does is [explain in more detail why it works].

Okay, got it?

Moving on…

Your second step is to [explain briefly what this step entails].

Here's where a lot of people make a very common mistake - they [explain the mistake]. And what happens is that [explain what sort of bad results the mistake causes, and WHY it causes those mistakes].

Now fortunately, this can all be fixed very easily… and there are a couple different ways to do it.

The first way is to [explain the first way to fix the problem]. [Explain the pros and cons of this particular solution.]

That's one possibility… but personally, I prefer to do it a slightly different way.

The second way [to avoid this mistake or make the process easier] is to [explain the second way to fix the problem]. Of course there are pros and cons with this method too. Namely, [explain the main pros and cons].

The reason why I prefer this method is because [explain why you use this particular method… and go into further detail as needed about how to use it. This may be a place where you mention a tool or product to make the particular process easier, which you'll then refer to again at the end of the webinar.]

So that all makes sense, right? So let's move onto the next step…

The third step you need to take in order to [get some result or complete some process] is to [explain what this third step is]. And specifically [give more specific instructions about how to complete this step].

Now this step can get a little tricky, because [explain why it can get a little tricky]. What I like to do is [explain a tip or trick you use to complete this step]. What ends up happening is [explain why this tip or trick works so well to get the desired result].

<Continue on, adding any other steps as needed to explain the process. With each step, offer instructions on how to complete the steps, tips or tricks to make it easier, tools or resources to make the process easier, and/or instructions for avoiding common mistakes.>

Whew – so that's your step by step process for [achieving some goal or completing some result].

Let's do a quick recap:

[Quickly list and summarize the steps that you just covered. To hold attention, you may offer additional tips and tricks in this section.]

Now as mentioned, one of the best ways to [avoid a specific problem or to generally make completing a part of the process more quickly and easily] is to use [some specific paid tool or resource]. << You are introducing the money maker here!!!

You've probably dealt with this before, right? [Explain the signs or symptoms of the problem. E.G. "You get plenty of traffic, but your list isn't growing at all."]

It feels [explain how terrible it feels/how frustrating it is when this happens].

Here's why this happens…

[Explain the reason why this problem keeps happening.]

Now here's the good news…

[Product Name] [explain exactly how it eliminates the problem].

And that's not all…

[Explain the main benefits of the product. Tell people why they should buy this product and what it does for them.]

If you want to [get some really great results], then you're going to want to use [Product Name] too. You can order yours now [explain how to order - e.g., offer a short link].

[Where applicable, give a strong reason to order now, such as a limited time discount or even just the possibility of a price jump. E.G., *"Plus if you hurry and order right now, you'll lock in the lowest price.*

I can't guarantee that the price won't go up overnight, so I strongly urge you to order now by [explain how] *so you don't miss this great deal."*]

Okay, sounds good?

I'm going to send a link to you right after we get through with this call, so check your email just a bit later.

For now, I'd like to thank everyone for attending this webinar. I hope you learned quite a bit about the best way to [get some result]. And I look forward to seeing you [on your blog, on social media, etc.]. Take care, and have a good night/Enjoy the rest of your day!

10 Fill-In-The-Blank Email Swipes For Pre-Webinar Excitement & Post-Webinar Sales

When you're planning a webinar, there are two things you need to do with your mailing lists:

1. Create pre-webinar excitement.
2. Generate post-webinar sales.

Below you'll find 10 email swipes you can use for both of these purposes.

Take a look...

Pre-Webinar Excitement Swipes

Note: Some of these emails you'll send out to your regular email lists, while others you'll send out to those who've already registered for your webinar. (You send emails to registrants because you want to keep registrants excited so that they attend.)

Email 1:
Have you ever wanted [to get some benefit]?

Hi [Name],

If you're like a lot of [type of niche people], then you're tired of [getting some bad result]. Seems like every time you try to [achieve some goal], you just end up [with some bad result].

Until now...

Because on [date and time], you're going to find out how to finally [get some awesome benefit]. And it's all free when you join the [name of webinar] webinar!

Here's how to sign up: [registration link]

Just look at what you'll discover during this free event:

- You'll find out the #1 way to [get some benefit]!
- You'll learn how to avoid the top [number] mistakes that plague most [type of people]
- Plus, you'll even discover the secret of [getting some good result]!

The webinar is coming up fast, so join now!

[sign off]

P.S. You're going to want to sign up right now, because there's limited seating and they're bound to go fast. Grab yours here: [registration link]

Email 2:

What are you doing [day and time, e.g., "Tuesday night"]?

Hi [Name],

If you've ever wanted to [get some good result], then you're going to want to spend an hour with [us] on [day] [time of day, e.g., "evening," "morning," "afternoon"]. That's because we're doing a free webinar, where we're sharing everything we know about [getting some specific benefit]!

Inside this jam-packed hour you'll discover [how to get some benefit]. You'll even get a surefire [tip/strategy/way] [to get some other benefit]. Plus, there will also be an opportunity at the end to get your [type of] questions answered!

An event like this doesn't come around very often, so click here [LINK] to join now!

[sign off]

P.S. There are only [number] seats available and they're going to go fast, so join now while you still can! Click here: [LINK]

Email 3:
There are only [number] webinar seats left…

Hi [Name],

I knew this [type of or name of] webinar would fill up fast, but I didn't think it would fill up THIS fast! As I write this, there are only [number] seats left - and there will be even fewer available by the time you read this!

Don't miss out - join this free event right now by clicking here: [link]

It's no wonder the seats are filling up fast. It's because [give a good reason - what is the MAIN benefit of this webinar]!

Plus, you're even going to [discover how to get some other benefit], WITHOUT [the typical unpleasant side effects/bad results that usually happen].

How is that possible? That's exactly what you'll find out during the free webinar, so register now at:

[link]

[sign off]

P.S. Set a reminder - the webinar is [date and time] … I'll see you there!

Email 4:
The best way to [get some benefit]?

Hi [Name],

You've probably tried to [get some benefit] many times over [the past days/weeks/months/years]. But every time you think you're finally getting it, [some bad thing happens].

You know what? You're not alone. And it's not your fault. Here's why…

[Explain why the reader keeps getting some bad result - something that isn't their fault, either because it's a factor out of their control or it's something no one has ever told them about.]

But there's a way to get around this problem. And that's by [explain briefly how to avoid the problem]. Simply put, it's the best way to [get some good result]!

So how does it all work? And how can you [start using this method] to [get great results for yourself]?

That's what you'll find out [day and time of webinar] during the free [Name of Webinar] webinar. Join now:

[link]

[sign off]

P.S. Only the first [number] who register now will get a seat at this free event, so click here to get started: [link]

Email 5:
It all starts tonight!

Hi [Name],

Just a reminder - the [type of] webinar starts tonight at [time]. You won't want to miss it, because [give the single best reason/benefit] why people will want to attend.

You can join in by [explain how to get on the call].

See you there!

[sign off]

P.S. Here's that link again: [webinar link]

Post-Webinar Sales Swipes

During the webinar you promoted some specific product or service. A few people probably purchased it right after the webinar ended. But for everyone else, you need to send a few follow ups to boost conversions and generate sales.

Check out these swipes...

Email 1:
Webinar replay is now available...

Hi [Name],

Wow - what a great webinar we had last night, where [attendees discovered how to get some great result]!

If you attended, then you're probably eager to watch it again. And if you didn't attend, then you're definitely going to want to catch the replay. The good news is that it's ready now, and you can watch it here for free:

[link to replay]

Attendees can't stop talking about the webinar. Almost everyone is [talking about some specific tip/secret shared during the webinar]. And no wonder - this [tip/secret is changing the way people approach some task] ... and people are getting amazing results!

So watch (or re-watch) the webinar right now at:

[link]

[sign off]

P.S. The people who are getting the BEST [type of] results are the ones who [are using some paid product or service]. You can get great results too by clicking here [link to promo] …

And if you hurry, you'll even [get some special discount offer], so click the link above now to check it out!

Email 2:
What's holding you back from [achieving some goal]?

Hi [Name],

Do you ever feel like you're struggling to [get a good niche-relevant result], while everyone else seems to make it look so easy?

If so, then you probably loved watching the webinar the other night, where we revealed the biggest factors [that hold you back from achieving your goal]. If you want to catch the replay, you can do so right here:

[link]

(By the way, that replay link isn't going to be available for free for too much longer, so be sure to watch it now while you still can.)

To quickly recap, there are [number] potential problems that can greatly affect your [type of] results:

1. [Describe the first problem.] [Explain briefly what the webinar said about getting around that problem.]

2. [Describe the second problem.] [Explain briefly what the webinar said about getting around that problem.]

3. [Describe the third problem.] [Explain briefly what the webinar said about getting around that problem.

Now most people find the third problem the most troublesome. And that's because [list a reason why it's such a sticky problem].

Now here's the good news…

You can virtually eliminate [any specific issues associated with this problem] when you use [Name of Product].

That's right, this [type of product] [provides some highly desirable benefit], without [having the user suffer with some undesired side effect/consequence]. Finally, now you too can [get a great result]!

Best of all?

If you act now, you can get a [number]% off discount on [Name of Product] when you order now using this link:

[link to product]

This very special offer ends soon, so grab it now while you still can!

[sign off]

P.S. You're going to love [Product Name] and the way it [delivers some benefit] - I guarantee it! So go ahead and order now and use it for a full 60 days. If you're not absolutely thrilled with your results, simply email me for a full and prompt refund.

Fair enough? Then order now at [link]…

Email 3:

The easy way [to avoid/get around some specific problem] …

Hi [Name],

Think about this for a moment…

Almost everyone who [has achieved some specific niche goal] has done it by [doing some very specific thing].

But up until now, it's been really difficult to [do that very specific thing]. That's because [list the reason why it's difficult to do that thing].

Now as you learned during the [Name of Webinar] webinar, there IS a way to make it easier than ever to [get around this problem].

The solution? You need to [do something in a specific way]. And that's exactly what [Name of Product] helps you do.

Order now, and in just minutes you'll discover:

- A surprisingly easy way to [get some result] - you'll kick yourself when you find out what it is!

- What the [type of experts/authorities in the niche] do when they want [to get some good result] - and how you can start doing it too to get great results!

- The #1 way to [get some awesome benefit] - almost no one knows about this amazing [secret/strategy/method/etc.]!

So, here's the bottom line…

If you want to start [getting some great result], then you need to do what the pros do and start using [Name of Product].

Click here to get started:

[link]

[sign off]

P.S. There's still time to get a [number]% off discount when you order [Name of Product]. But this special offer ends soon, so grab your savings at the following link while you still can: [link]

Email 4:
Here's what others are saying about [Product Name]…

Hi [Name],

There's a lot of excitement right now in [type of niche] circles about [Name of Product]. And if you watched the [Name of Webinar] webinar the other night, you're probably pretty excited too.

But there's something else on a lot of people's minds. Namely, does [Name of Product] REALLY work? Does it really [get some good result]?

The short answer: A resounding YES.

In fact, we're so sure that you're going to love your results, that we've backed the product with an iron-clad, 60-day money back guarantee. If you're not totally thrilled with [Name of Product], all you have to do is let us know so we can offer you a prompt and cheerful full refund.

But we're not the only ones who think this product is the best way to [get some great result]. Our customers are raving too.

Just take a look at what [name] from [location] says about [Name of Product]:

[Insert one of your strongest testimonials - preferably one that talks about the actual results the testimonial giver received.]

And he/she isn't the only one who's getting great results. Check this out:

[Insert another strong testimonial]

Or how about this…

[Name of testimonial giver] didn't even think it was possible for [him/her] to get great results, because [list why they didn't think it was possible]. But just look at what happened:

[Insert another strong testimonial.]

You can get great results like this too. Click here to get started:

[link]

[sign off]

P.S. Hurry and order now while you can still get yourself a special price! Click here: [link]

Email 5:
Time is running out on a great deal…

Hi [Name],

Just a heads up that the special offer for [some discount or other great deal] [Name of Product] is about to expire. You'll want to snatch it up while you still can right here:

[link]

Simply put, this [type of or name of product] is the best way to [get some really good benefit]. That's because [list a reason why this product is better than other solutions on the market - basically, offer the USP (unique selling proposition) here].

But don't take my word for it - order now risk free at:

[link]

And hurry because the special discount price ends [list when it ends]!

[sign off]

P.S. Yes, [Product Name] is worth every penny even when you pay full price. But why pay more when you don’t have to? Order now to get yourself a big discount: [ink]

5 Fill-In-The-Blank Landing Page Opt-In Templates For Getting Lots Of Sign-Ups

So, imagine this...

You're all excited about your webinar. You have these visions of people signing up like crazy until they fill every single one of your seats. And you imagine a webinar full of eager viewers who're sitting there with their credit cards in hand, ready to buy whatever you're promoting.

But the reality?

You struggle to get even a handful of signups.

Yikes.

Don't let this happen to you.

The first step to avoid this is to create a webinar that people really want to attend (which we've talked about elsewhere).

The second step is to create an opt-in page that gets people signing up for your webinar like crazy. And that's exactly what you get below with these five surefire opt-in templates.

Take a look...

Template 1

Who Else Wants To [Get Some Great Result]?

Free [Type Of] Webinar Shows You How The ["Pros" Or Similar Descriptor] [Get Some Great Result] - And How You Can Too!

Every day, [some big number—dozens/hundreds/thousands] of people try to [get some good result]. And every day, the vast majority of them will fail.

Sound familiar?

Maybe you've tried to [get some good result] before too, but you just ended up [getting some bad result]. It feels like a kick in the gut when that happens. It makes you want to throw in the towel and just forget about trying to [achieve some result].

But not so fast…

Maybe the reason [you're not getting a good result] is because [of some specific factor]. Maybe no one has ever told you the right way to [complete some task].

Until now…

Introducing the [Name of Webinar] Webinar: a FREE event where you'll finally discover the secrets of [getting some great result]!

We're leaving no stone uncovered when it comes to [getting a good result]. During the course of this jam-packed hour, you'll discover:

- Which [number] [tools/resources] everyone who wants to [get some result] ought to be using. (Hint: you'll be surprised at how easy it is to [get a result] when you're using [these tools]!)

- The #1 reason why the vast majority of [type of people] will NEVER [get some good result] - and the quick and easy way you can avoid the same fate!

- A simple [number]-step process for [getting some great result]!

And much, much more. Plus, you'll even get a chance to ask your toughest [type of] questions!

The webinar happens on [date and time], and it's totally free. But seating is strictly limited, so you need to register now to guarantee a seat for this in-demand webinar!

So don't delay - fill out the form below now to get registered:

[insert opt-in form]

… and I'll see you [day] at [time]!

[sign off]

P.S. You're going to kick yourself if you miss this rare event, so hurry and reserve your seat now!

Template 2

Eye-Opening Webinar Reveals the Startling Secrets Of [Getting Some Good Niche-Relevant Result]!

Reserve your seat now before someone else does…

Attention [Type of People - e.g., "Marketers" or "Allergy Sufferers"] …

Do you ever [name some sign or symptom of a problem]?

Do you sometimes feel [name another sign of a problem]?

Have you ever noticed [insert still another sign/symptom of a problem]?

If so, you're not alone. Every day, people just like you all around the planet are desperately looking for [a way to get some good result] - and they're coming up empty handed.

[Some common strategy] doesn't work because you just end up [getting some undesired result].

[Another common strategy] also tends to be disappointing. After all, how many times have you tried to [get a good result using this strategy], but [something bad happened instead]?

Happens all the time, and not just to you.

But here's the good news…

You CAN [start getting some good result] - and you'll find out how on [date and time] during a special hour-long webinar entitled, "[Name of Webinar]."

A chance like this doesn't come around very often. During this live event you'll discover:

- Why the vast majority of people will fail when they try to [achieve some result] - and how you can turn the tables in your favor!

- The quickest and easiest way to [get some good result] - and it has NOTHING to do with [some common thing most people would assume].

- The very best way to [get some great result].

And much, much more! By the time you hang up, you'll know exactly how to [get some great result]!

But there's a catch…

There are only [number] of virtual seats available for this special webinar, and you know they're going to go super-fast. So, reserve yours now using the form below:

[opt in form]

And I'll see you [date and time] at the webinar!

[sign off]

P.S. Don't delay - reserve your seat now before they're all gone!

Template 3

Want [to get a great result]?

Then reserve your seat now to this year's hottest [type of] webinar!

If you've ever wanted to [get some good result], then this is the webinar you've been waiting for. That's because we've lined up [number] of the niche's top [type of] experts to give you the truth, the whole truth, and nothing but the truth about [topic]!

Take a look at the guest panel:

[Guest Expert #1's Name] [Guest's Name] comes to this webinar with over [number] years of experience [in some particular field or achieving some particular result]. Now you can tap into [Name's] expertise, as [he/she] shares [describe the benefits of what this expert will be sharing.]

[Guest Expert #2's Name] [Do the same as above - short bio + what the guest is sharing.]

[Insert other guest experts as needed.]

It's rare to get so many top-shelf [type of] experts all in one place, so this is one webinar you don't want to miss! By the time this webinar ends, you'll [know exactly how to achieve some specific result]!

It all happens [date and time of the webinar]. So reserve your virtual seat now using the form below:

[opt-in form]

And hurry, because seating is strictly limited to [number] - and you know these spots are going to go fast!

Template 4

Are You Making These [Type Of] Mistakes?

Free webinar shows you how to avoid the [costly/time-consuming] mistakes that plague most [types of people]!

If you're just getting started [trying to achieve some result], then you're bound to make a lot of mistakes. This is especially true if you're trying to figure it all out on your own.

But here's the thing…

There are a lot of people who've learned about [some topic] the hard way, but spending [a lot of time] and [a lot of money]. They've made a ton of mistakes. They've had setbacks. They've been frustrated to the point where they wanted to give up.

And you know what? You can learn from their mistakes.

Point is, you don't need to go making the same mistakes as everyone else…

If you want to [get some good result] faster, easier, and cheaper than almost everyone else, then you're going to want to jump on this free webinar [at date and time]!

That's right, you're going to find out how to avoid all those costly mistakes, so that you can finally [get a great result]! Take a look at what all we'll cover:

- You'll learn how to avoid the top [number] common [type of] mistakes - as soon as you know this information, you'll save yourself a ton of time and money!

- You'll find out how to save yourself over [$ amount] [on the cost of some common type of niche cost, such as "gym fees" or "web hosting fees"]!

- You'll get a super-easy way to [get some good benefit] - you'll be amazed that you never heard about this before!

- You'll find out the REAL secret of [getting some result] - and trust me, it's not what you think!

And much, much more - this hour-long webinar is going to be spilling over with our best tips and tricks for [getting a great result]! Plus, you'll get the opportunity to get answers to your toughest [type of] questions at the end of the webinar!

But heads up…

Only [number] people can attend this FREE webinar [on date and time]: Will you be one of the lucky few?

I wish there was room enough on this webinar for everyone who needed to learn about [these types of secrets] - but there's not. And that means there's a very good chance you could get left out.

So what you want to do is sign up using the form below to reserve your spot right ow - this will guarantee you access to the live webinar, plus you'll even get access to the replay to watch whenever you please. Fill out the form below now:

[opt in form]

Then start thinking about the kinds of questions you want to ask!

See you [date and time] - don’t be late because every minute of this webinar is going to be spilling over with solid-gold tips and tricks!

Template 5

Special Guest Expert [Name of Expert] Explains [How To Get Some Awesome Niche Result] - And You Can Watch Live for FREE!

Mark your calendars for [date and time] so you can attend this very rare webinar event!

If you know anything about [niche topic], then you've probably heard of [guest expert's name]. That's because [name] is considered the foremost expert on [some topic or getting some result]. And since [he/she] as [number] years of experience producing great results, you can bet people listen when [name] talks.

Which brings us to the exciting announcement…

YOU can hear [name] talk for FREE on [date and time] at a very special [topic/type of] webinar!

[Name] is in high demand in [niche] circles, so this is a very rare opportunity. Most people who are [trying to get some result] pay upwards of [some dollar amount] for just one hour of [guest expert's] time. And if you've ever looked into attending [his or her] seminars, then you know tickets start at [price].

Any time you can hear [name] talk is well worth the asking price… But on [date] you can attend this [dollar amount… estimated value] webinar for FREE!

An opportunity like this doesn't come around very often, so reserve your seat right now using the form below:

[Insert opt-in form.]

Here's a sneak peek at what you'll discover during this exciting live event:

- [Guest Name] will reveal the single biggest strategy [he/she] uses every day to [get some good result] - and how you can put it to work to get good results for you too!

- You'll get [Name's] complete step-by-step system for [getting a good result] - this system really simplifies the entire process!

- You'll find out how to [get some good result], even if you don't [have some typical prerequisite skills or experience]!

- You'll find out the exact [tools/resources] [guest expert] uses to [get a good result] - just imagine what they can do for you!

Plus, there will also be an opportunity to ask questions at the end of the webinar.

And once the webinar is over, you'll also get these fantastic bonuses:

- Unlimited access to the webinar replay - you can watch it again any time that you like!

- A complete text transcript that you're sure to refer to again and again!

- A webinar summary with timestamps, so you can easily hop around to the topics and sections that you most want to watch again!

- [Some tool that the guest expert is handing out, such as a worksheet, checklist, templates, etc.].

- [Any other bonuses.]

The virtual seating for this event is going to fill up super-fast, so reserve your place on this webinar now by filling in the form below:

[Insert opt-in form again.]

And I'll see you [date and time], with special guest [Name]!

How To Create Amazing Presentation Slides For Webinars

If you're doing a slide-presentation webinar, then one part of the equation you need to snap into place is your script.

We've talked about that elsewhere in this toolkit, so now let's turn our attention to the second part of the equation: **the slides.**

If you get this part wrong, you're going to have people slumping over in boredom as they watch your webinar. That's why you want to create amazing slides that will keep your audience hooked, engaged and paying attention.

How do you create these sorts of slides?

Simple – by using this guide.

Take a look…

Step 1: Get Slide Presentation Software

The first thing you need to do is select the software you'll use to create your slide presentation.

The old standby is PowerPoint.

Possibly you already have this on your computer if you have a Windows system and the Office Suite installed.

If not, you can pick it up here:
https://www.microsoft.com/en-us/store/d/powerpoint-2016/cfq7ttc0k5ct.

There are some other possibilities.

Here are several PowerPoint alternatives for you to consider:

- www.prezi.com
- www.powtoon.com
- www.haikudeck.com
- Camtasia Studio
  https://www.techsmith.com/camtasia.html.
  This is a suite which includes screen-presentation, screen recording and editing software.

If you need still other options, then search Google for "PowerPoint alternatives" or "slide presentation software."

Step 2: Outline Your Slides

Your next step is to create an outline and rough draft for your slides. In other words, before you actually start creating slides, you should know exactly how many slides you'll have and roughly what will appear on each slide.

Your first slide will be the title slide, which will show the title (and subtitle) of the webinar alongside your name and any other relevant information.

The next one to three slides will show a little information about you. How much you tell depends on the level of credibility you need to build with your audience.

Keep in mind that there is a fine line here – on the one hand, you want people to know why they should trust you. On the other hand, you don't want to talk about yourself too much, because people essentially don't care. So use the absolute minimum amount of time required to build credibility – in some cases, that may just be 20 or 30 seconds in an hour-long presentation.

Next, now you need to draft slides for the "meat" of your presentation. This can vary widely depending on what you're presenting and how quickly you talk.

But here are a few guidelines:

- A general rule of thumb is one slide per minute. You may want to time yourself speaking (which will likely be 150 words per minute or so) to get an idea of how much ground you can cover in a minute.

- For "heavy" topics, you may spend longer on a particular slide. However, don't spend more than two or so minutes on a slide, as your audience will get bored. Instead, create another supporting slide in order to convey the information.

- For light topics (such as stories), you can flip through the slides more quickly to keep your audience engaged.

As you create your slides, think of how to break your presentation into "sections." You can then start each section with an "overview" slide, and then break down and take a closer look at each point from the overview slide.

For example, if you're talking about weight loss, you might start the presentation by letting people know they'll be learning about three areas: Nutrition, Exercise and Motivation. **This is your overview slide.**

Next, you'd go into each of those three subtopics. You might start the nutrition topic by presenting another overview of these subtopics, such as "Protein," "Carbs" and "Essential Fats."

You'd then start with the "Protein" topic and show a collection of slides on that topic. Next you'd cover the "Carbs" topic with a series of slides. Same thing with the "Essential Fats" topic.

At this point, you may then show a "Recap" slide where you summarize the three or so biggest takeaways from the "Protein" topic.

Then you'd move to the "Carbs" topic, where again you'd show an overview of what you'll cover in that section.

You get the idea.

So in order to put together a draft of your slides, you'll need to outline your entire presentation, and then think about the types of slides that will enhance your message.

Remember that your slide should enhance your verbal presentation, not compete with it.

Don't make people choose between reading something on your slide or listening to your words, which happens when the text on a slide is radically different than what you're saying. In other words, the slides should complement the oral part of the presentation.

So let's move to the next step...

Step 3: Create The Slides

Now that you've outlined your entire presentation, including creating a draft of your slides, it's time to actually create them.

There are two main things you'll be inserting into your slides: text and graphics. Sometimes you'll have a text-only slide, sometimes it will be a graphics-only slide, and in other cases you'll have a slide consisting of both text and graphics.

Let's look at these two parts separately...

The Graphics

You can use graphics on your slides in multiple ways, including:

- As an illustration to demonstrate something. For example, if your slide is talking about the proper position to do a barbell squat, then you might include an illustration or photo that depicts the correct position.

- Helpful graphics. If you're talking about something or someone that some people may be unfamiliar with, you can post a photo or illustration. For example, if you're talking about the difference between a long-haired Chihuahua and Pomeranian, you might include side-by-side photos to show the differences.

- To simply compliment the presentation. For example, let's suppose you're talking about dog training. When you're going through your introduction, you may simply show a picture of one or more cute dogs (even better if the dogs belong to you).

- To depict something humorous. One way to keep the audience engaged is with humor, and a comic or meme is one way to inject this humor.

- To show a visual representation of data. For example, if you're going over the statistics for some event, you might show a pie chart or similar item that lets people take in and absorb the data quickly.

In short, you can use your graphics to enhance the presentation, increase engagement, and keep your viewers watching.

So how do you create these graphics? You have three main options:

Option 1 is to hire someone to do it for you.

If you have zero graphical skills, this is a good option because you'll get a better end result than you'd be able to do on your own. You can find someone on a freelancing site such as UpWork.com. Or if you need very simple graphics, you might even find someone to do it for your on Fiverr.com.

Option 2 is to purchase suitable graphics.
This is a great option if you want professional photos or graphics, but all you really need is something fairly generic (such as a photo of a dog swimming, for example).

For this option, you can purchase stock photos and other graphics on sites such as:

- www.depositphotos.com
- www.istockphoto.com
- www.bigstockphoto.com

Option 3 is to create them yourself.
You can either tweak stock photos or create graphics from scratch if you have the skills. You might choose a popular graphics-editing program such as Photoshop, or an alternative such as:

- www.pixlr.com
- www.gimp.org
- www.canva.com

Next…

The Text

As mentioned before, sometimes you may have text-only slides, and other times you may opt to include both text and graphics.

Keep these best practices in mind:

- Place one idea on each slide. In other words, your text should highlight the main point of whatever you're talking about at the moment, but this text shouldn't be too wordy.

  For example, if you're offering copywriting tips, one of your slides may simply state, "Create attention-driven, curiosity arousing headlines." Your narration will explain this concept in more detail, and then you can later present slides with headline templates and examples that incorporate these ideas.

- Use a large, readable font. Don't try to be clever with "cutesy" fonts. Stick to the common fonts that are easy to read, such as Tahoma, Arial and Verdana.

- Make use of bulleted list. If you have multiple points to cover on one slide, use bulleted lists. For example, perhaps you're listing the three best web hosts. You can list all three of these in a bulleted list, which is much easier to read than in paragraph format.

And finally...

Step 4: Put It All Together

So now that you know how to create the text and graphics for your slides, let's kick up the awesomeness. Take note of these tips and tricks:

- Point graphics towards the text. People naturally tend to look in the direction the subject of a photo is looking. So for example, if you have a photo of a dog that's oriented slightly in one direction, then your text should be wear the dog's nose/eyes are pointing. The same goes for humans and any other animal.

    TIP: This applies to non-human/animal objects too. For example, if you have a photo of a car, then people will naturally look from the back end of the car to the front... and beyond (as that is typically the direction a car would travel). So put the text next to the headlights of a car.

    Point is, look at all your graphics to determine where it "points" – and then put your text where the object, human or other animal is "pointing" or looking.

- Highlight important parts of a graphic. If you're showing something like a screenshot, then use an arrow to point to the part of the graphic you want your viewers to focus on.

    TIP: In general, you should use uncluttered, simple graphics that your viewer can "absorb" within a second. The above tip only applies to when you absolutely need to show a "cluttered" graphic, such as a screenshot where you're showing people how to access a specific feature in a software's dashboard.

- Be careful with transitions. Your slide-presentation software will give you different options for having slides enter and exit the screen. If you use these, try to be consistent and use the same or similar transitions throughout. Your presentation itself should wow your viewers, not your transitions.

- Consider background music. If you watch professional commercials or slide presentations, you'll notice that there is always an upbeat bit of music playing softly in the background. If you're doing voice-cover narration, then you'll enhance your presentation by adding music (assuming the music is soft and doesn't overpower the narration). If you're not doing a voice-over (slide presentation only, which isn't recommended for a webinar), then you'll definitely want music.

- Be consistent. Each slide should look like it's part of the same presentation. If you try to hold interest by creating slides that have a different feel with different fonts, colors and so on, the strategy may backfire. It can feel jarring to the viewer rather aesthetically pleasing.

Let's wrap things up…

Conclusion

So there you have it – a step-by-step guide for creating awesome slides for your webinar!

If you really want to create an awesome presentation, then spend time on YouTube.com and SlideShare.net watching other peoples' popular presentations.

Take note of the following:

- The overall pacing of the presentation.
- How they keep you engaged.
- The tone and enthusiasm of the speaker.
- How the slides are constructed (graphics only, text only, or text and graphics).

In short, reverse engineer great presentations, and then model yours after these popular slide-shares!

Webinar Worksheets:

5 Worksheets To Plan A Successful Webinar

One of the keys to creating a successful webinar is to plan every step of it carefully. The more you know about the who, what, how and why of your webinar, the better your overall end product will be.

Want to kick start your planning?

Then use these five worksheets…

Worksheet 1: Who is your audience?

In order to create a webinar that really resonates with your audience, as well as create marketing that appeals to them, you need to understand your audience as much as possible. This worksheet helps you do that in two steps. Let's get started...

Step 1: Research Your Audience

First, you need to do a little legwork in order to learn more about your audience. As you go through these steps, take notes on what you're learning, as you'll need this information to complete the next step.

Here are the research steps:

- Find out what your audience is buying. This is a good predictor of whether they'll attend your free webinar and/or purchase the products. To do this, search for your niche keywords in marketplaces such as Amazon.com, ClickBank.com and JvZoo.com. (Take note of the bestsellers, and any topic where there are multiple competing products – these are all evidence of an in-demand topic.)

- See what topics are popular in niche communities. Check social media, blogs, forums and other communities to see which topics your audience is eager to know more about.

- Look at what types of webinars your competitors are holding. Check the popularity if possible (e.g., if your competitors mention how many people were on a call).

- Use keyword tools like WordTracker to find out what's popular. Search for your keywords and see what types of searches your market is doing.

- Search Google for your niche keywords. If you search for your broad keywords (like "dog training"), you'll get a sense of what types of information products your competitors are selling. If you search for your broad keywords alongside the word "webinar" (e.g., "dog training webinar"), you'll learn more about what types of webinars are popular in the niche.

- Ask your market. Survey them to find out more about their demographics, what they want, and whether they attend webinars.

- Search for your market demographics in Google. E.G., "dog owner demographics." Then learn as much as you can about your audience but be sure to only focus on reputable sources of data (such as data from government organizations, research institutions and similar).

- Spend time talking to your audience. This will give you a better insight into what they want. You can do this online via social media and other communities, or even offline by attending niche-relevant meetings.

Step 2: Profile Your Audience

Now that you've collected all this information, it's time to write down as much as you know about your audience.

Fill in these audience demographics and interests based on your research:

- Age:
- Gender:
- Location:
- Income:
- Educational level:

- How do they spend their disposable income?
- How much money do they spend on niche items?
- What are their biggest problems in the niche?
- What sorts of solutions are they looking for?
- What types of products are they already buying/using?
- What are the problems with solutions on the market?
- What are the strengths of these types of solutions?
- What information do they need to have better success in the niche?
- Do they attend webinars? If not, why not?
- What sort of device do they use to access the web?
- Does this market use any type of specific jargon?
- What else do you know about this market?

In summary…

If you fill in all of the information above about your audience, you'll have a good insight how to best connect with your audience and create webinars (and sell products) based on the topics that matter to them the most!

Worksheet 2: Why are you doing a webinar?

Before you start planning your webinar, you need to get very clear about WHY you're doing it. That is, what are your goals? What do you hope to accomplish? Once you're able to answer those questions, then you'll be able to plan a webinar that helps you achieve your goals. Use this worksheet to get started...

There are many reasons to do a webinar.

Start by circling all of the following reasons that interest you:

- Build your mailing list.
- Generate sales on the backend.
- Create a lead magnet or even paid product for later use.
- Establish your expertise/authority in the niche.
- Build your branding.
- Develop better relationships with JV partners.
- Give your loyal customers a bonus product.
- Introduce yourself to new prospects in the niche.
- Build relationships with prospects and customers.
- Offer group coaching to your audience.
- List any other reasons that interest you:

You've probably circled a few different reasons why you'd like to do a webinar. However, you need to focus on just one PRIMARY reason.

Ask yourself these questions:

- Which of the reasons for doing a webinar will BEST support your overall business goals?
- Which of the reasons for doing a webinar are BEST served by doing a webinar (versus doing some other task).

Now with the answers to the above two questions in mind, answer the following questions:

- What is your PRIMARY reason for doing this webinar? (Choose just one.)
- What EXACTLY do you hope to accomplish by doing this webinar? Be as specific as possible. For example, if you want to build a list, then detail how many new subscribers you'd like to attract to this list and how you'd like to monetize the list.
- What are your top secondary reasons for doing this webinar? List/rank them in order of importance.
- List exactly what you hope to accomplish in terms of these secondary goals. Again, be as specific and detailed as possible.

What you'll do now is create a webinar that's mainly focused on your primary goal. If it's possible, you'll also integrate factors into your webinar to achieve your secondary goals.
For example, if your primary goal is to build a list and your secondary goal is to generate sales on the backend, those are completely compatible goals. So that means you can work on both of them together.

On the other hand, if your primary goal is to help out a JV partner and your secondary goal is to generate sales of your own product on the backend, those two goals aren't necessarily compatible (as you'd be focusing on selling your JV partner's product, not yours). So in that case, be sure you are designing your webinar around your primary goal.

Worksheet 3: What will you sell on the backend?

In most cases, you're going to sell a product on the backend of your webinar. It's important to pick your product out FIRST, because knowing what you're selling will help you design your webinar. (Which you'll plan in Worksheet #4.)

For now, let's focus on what you're selling.

What product do you intend to sell?

Is this your own product or an affiliate product?

- If it's an affiliate product, what sort of commission rate do you receive?

- If it's your own product, what will you sell on the backend of this product? In other words, what does your sales funnel look like?

What is the price of this product? (This is important to know, because a higher price product generally requires more selling than a "no brainer" tripwire product.)

Is your audience already familiar with products like this?

Is your audience familiar with this SPECIFIC type of product?

What sort of conversion rate does the sales letter usually return?

What are the main benefits of this product?

What is the unique selling proposition of this product?

Are you going to extend any special offers to boost sales? If so, what sort of special offers? (Keep in mind that if you offer a limited-time discount, then your webinar won't exactly be evergreen unless you edit that part of the webinar.)

In what other ways can you create urgency to help boost sales?

How will you sell this product during the webinar? In other words, how will you warm up (presell) your audience? Be as specific as possible.

For example, will you presell by:

- Using fear-logic-gain?
- Focusing on benefits, like a typical sales letter?
- Using story-telling selling?
- Offering proof, such as case studies, testimonials, photos, videos, etc.?
- Demonstrating the product?

And so on. You may incorporate methods for preselling (or all of them). Just be clear about what methods you intend to use, and why you intend to use those methods.

How will you promote the product outside of the webinar itself?

For example:

- On the webinar registration thank you page.
- Inside the pre-webinar emails.
- Inside the post-webinar emails.
- Inside emails your joint venture partners send.
- Other places such as your blog or social media.
- Inside any webinar handouts.

And so on. List all that apply. Basically, you want to create a mini marketing plan here for promoting your backend product.

In Summary...

The planning you do now will help you create a better webinar. So even though it takes a little time upfront to plan your product and choose the best one to promote, it's well worth the extra sales you'll get on the backend!

Worksheet 4: What content for your webinar?

If you've been doing these worksheets in order, then at this point you know what you're selling on the backend of your webinar and how you intend to sell it. That's good, because now you can use that information to help you design the meat of your webinar.

Use this worksheet to plan your webinar content...

What product are you selling on the backend of your webinar?

What type of webinar content would BEST help you sell this content? In other words, how will you create a useful-yet-incomplete webinar that impresses prospects and helps you presell the product?

Examples:

- An overview of a step-by-step process. This works well for selling an in-depth information product on the backend. For example, give an overview of how to win a bodybuilding competition, and then sell an in-depth guide on the backend.

- In-depth instruction on PART of a process. You can sell tools, physical products, or information products on the backend. For example, show people how to set up a membership site, and then sell a guide that shows people how to market and monetize their membership site.

- Complete step-by-step instructions for a process. This works well for selling related tools. For example, offer complete instructions for creating a sales letter, and then sell sales letter templates and swipes on the backend.

- Tips and tools webinar. This works well for selling information products, the tools you mention during the webinar or similar items. For example, you might offer tips for setting up a mailing list, with one of your tips being to secure a good email service provider – and then you could recommend a specific service on the backend.

- Guest expert. This is a good way to sell an affiliate product by interviewing the vendor.

- Case study. This is a good way to sell most any type of product, especially one that your market may be a little skeptical about, and/or one that's higher priced and requires a little more proof in order to move prospects towards the order button.

This is not an exhaustive list of the ways to present your webinar.

Other examples include a product review, product demonstration, etc.

What you need to do at this point is decide the BEST format for your webinar.

Once you decide on the format that will best help you presell your backend product, then consider how you'll structure your webinar. Which format works best you're your overall structure?

Specifically:

- Talking head webinar?
- Product demo?
- Whiteboard webinar?
- Slide-share presentation?
- Guest expert (talking head)?

How long will your webinar be?

Will you accept questions during the webinar?

Now create an outline for your webinar. What specific topics do you absolutely need to cover?

> TIP: You'll probably speak at the rate of 150 words or so per minute. Time yourself to find out your presentation rate. This will help you determine how much you can actually cover during the time you've allotted for the webinar.

What topics do you HOPE to cover, yet they aren't absolutely required?

If you have a guest expert or joint venture partner on the call, then what is their input regarding the topics they'd like to cover?

Does your webinar naturally lead to the paid promotion? In other words, is it a smooth transition from the webinar content to the pitch part of the webinar?

Do you plan to create an "evergreen" webinar? If so, check your rough draft script to be sure you don't mention anything that will date the content (that includes offering limited-time discounts or similar special offers on your backend product).

How do you plan to keep people engaged during the webinar? Be as specific as possible here. Examples:

- Interacting with viewers before the webinar to build rapport.
- Interacting with viewers during the webinar, such as by fielding questions.
- Using an enthusiastic tone of voice.
- Telling relevant stories to emotionally engage viewers.
- Focusing on THEM (their problems and how you can solve them).

(And so on.)

Conclusion

If you answer all the questions above and think carefully through these issues, you'll end up with an engaging webinar that does a great job of preselling your backend product!

Worksheet 5: How will you position your webinar?

You've got this great idea for a webinar. You've done your market research, so you know it's an in-demand topic. But before you start advertising it, you need to position it in a way that really gets your target market's attention, attracts them and fills your webinar seats.

That's what this worksheet helps you do...

Positioning Your Webinar

What you're doing here is creating a USP (unique selling proposition). This is a statement that tells your prospective attendees WHY they should attend your webinar. (After all, they could be attending your competitor's webinar instead or doing something entirely different with their time.)

Your USP tells them why your webinar is different and better than other webinars and information products in the niche.

So, what you need to do first is determine all the main benefits of your webinar. In other words, list all the reasons why people should attend.

What will they learn?
What will they get out of the webinar?

Don't limit your list at this point – just write down every single thing you can think of.

Secondly, think of the ways that your webinar is somehow different from other webinars.

For example:

- Do you have some unique qualifications to teach this webinar (a college degree, a large amount of experience in the niche, proven results with a lot of clients, a bestselling product, awards or accolades in the niche, etc.)?

- Do any of your guest experts have any sort of unique qualification?

- Does your webinar teach something completely new? (Or even just a new twist on an old method?)

- Is your webinar a "first" in some category? Or is your webinar, your method or you the "original" in some category?

- Do you offer some unique benefit that people can't find anywhere else?

- What else can you think of that may set you, your methods or your webinar apart from others?

Next, you need to look at your competitors' offerings and determine what USPs they're using to position their webinars (and other lead magnets).

> TIP: Sometimes you'll find this information in their slogans. Sometimes you'll find it embedded in a sales page. Some marketers make their USPs very clear, while others do not.

Next, now you need find out where your potential USPs overlap with your competitors' existing USPs. For obvious reasons, you don't want to position yourself and your webinars the same way in your market as your competitors. At this point you'll now have a "short list" of potential USPs. What you need to do next is determine which of these prospective USPs are of interest to your market. In other words, which ones do they really value?

You'll pick the USP that your market not only highly values, but also one where you have a lot of strength (i.e., one where you clearly stand out from the competition).

Finally, now you need to create a succinct statement that highlights your USP.

For an idea about how to craft these statements, just look to how big companies tend to do it.

Here are real-life examples:

- Better pizza. Better ingredients. Papa Johns.
- Fly the friendly skies.
- We try harder.
- When it absolutely, positively has to be there overnight.
- Mountain grown.
- The low-price leader.

You can see those are various USPs based on different factors, ranging from pricing to customer service to how the product is made. Obviously, not all of these factors are applicable to your webinars.

Nonetheless, these examples show you how to create a succinct statement.

Conclusion

Chances are, there is a lot of noise in your market as marketers compete with each other to fill their webinar seats and sell their products.

You can get a bigger share of the market simply by creating a USP, which tells your market WHY they should attend your webinar. After all, **your prospect's time is their most valuable asset** – so you need to do everything you can to get them to agree to give up a bit of their time to attend your webinar and crafting a USP is a great start!

- Bonus Section -

Boost Your Presentation Skills Printouts

CONFIDENCE

MINDSET

1. **ACTION FEEDS CONFIDENCE**
   The more action you take in life, the more power you have to break through fears. Express: Create, make, and do!
2. **FAKING IT LEADS TO BECOMING IT**
   You can't wait to reach mastery - you have to act as-if <u>before</u> you think you can, and as you do, you will achieve mastery
3. **YOUR WORDS HAVE IMMENSE POWER**
   Words can effect you in two ways: 1) They can point you to your power 2) When said out loud, they <u>give</u> you power!
4. **YOU'RE AS POWERFUL AS YOU THINK**
   If you think you can do a thing or think you can't do a thing, you're right. - **Henry Ford**
5. **HOW YOU USE YOUR BODY IS KEY**
   How you use your body affects how you think and feel - how you think and feels affects your sense of personal power
6. **YOU'RE BUILDING A MUSCLE**
   Like building a muscle, when it comes to building your confidence, it takes time, it's hard work/pain, and consistency is key
7. **SMALL ACTIONS CREATE MOMENTUM**
   Becoming confident will be easier if you focus on making small, doable changes instead of big and overwhelming changes
8. **BEING WRONG IS OK**
   Being invincible isn't the goal - you want to make mistakes and own them...learn to be OK with being wrong
9. **YOU MUST BECOME CONFIDENCE**
   Confidence is more than a strategy, it needs to be part of your identity - you want to raise your confidence 'thermostat'
10. **OTHERS CARE LESS THAN YOU THINK**
    We probably wouldn't worry about what people think of us if we could know how seldom they do. - **Olin Miller**

ACTIONS: I WILL...

PRACTICE WHAT IF...UP!
Change your focus from failure to success

POWER POSE
Stand & feel confident for 2 minutes

PRACTICE FREESTYLE EXPRESSION
Generate confidence by speaking out loud

SHOW CONFIDENCE IN SMALL WAYS
Focus on small steps instead of giant leaps

RELEASE NERVOUS ENERGY
Minimize the energy that destroys confidence

DRESS CONFIDENTLY
Look confident to feel confident

IDENTIFY & TRACK YOUR SMALL WINS
Keep a record of successes to build your confidence

TUNE INTO & ADJUST YOUR BODY LANGUAGE
Occasionally your body language

ELIMINATE NERVOUS HABITS
Get rid of nervous behaviors

VISUALIZE - MENTALLY REHEARSE
Experience winning, in advance

BE SPONTANEOUS
Train yourself to break through your fear barriers

GET MOVING!
Become a physical force of power and energy

SPEAK SLOWLY
Control your speaking to control your anxiety

SPEAK **SLOWLY**

KEY IDEA:
Control your speaking to control your anxiety

DISCUSSION

Anxious energy speeds up your speech

- Nervous energy needs released - either through rapid muscle movements or a fast tongue
- Speak too fast and you reveal your fear to others

Speaking slowly: The antidote to anxiety

- Anxiety can speed up your speech - slowing down your speech can minimize anxiety
- It fools your brain into believing you're OK
- You breathe better - leads to being calm
- You have more time to think before you speak

How to speak slowly

- Pay attention - tune into how you speak
- As you tune in, focus on slowing down
- Articulate your words - be slow, deliberate, and specific
- Pause occasionally
- Breathe!

It won't be weird

- What seems like slow and boring to you conveys calm and confidence to others

IMPLEMENTATION

When I...

- Speak

Then I will...

- Tune in to the speed of my speaking and slow down

CHALLENGE: For the next 7-30 days, I challenge myself to:

- Speak slower than what seems normal, especially in situations that cause me anxiety

RELEASE
NERVOUS ENERGY

KEY IDEA:
Minimize the energy that destroys confidence

DISCUSSION

Nervousness is unreleased energy

- Fight-or-flight energy ignited by a release of adrenaline with nowhere to go:
  - Your heart rate speeds up
  - Your muscles get jittery
  - You begin to sweat

Nervousness CAN be controlled

- You're not genetically inclined to feel nervous
- It's possible to minimize or even eliminate it

Your body is your best weapon

- You rarely talk yourself out of nervousness
- Use your body to release the nervous energy

3 simple ways to release nervous energy

- Take 3 deep breaths
- Clench (fists and toes) and release
- Walk, jump around, or stretch - get moving
- OPTIONAL: Say a powerful affirmation

IMPLEMENTATION

When I...

- Feel nervous

Then I will...

- Take 3 deep breaths
- Clench and release
- Walk, jump around, or stretch - get moving

PRACTICE
WHAT IF... UP!

KEY IDEA:
Change your focus from failure to success

DISCUSSION

If you are going to doubt something, doubt your limits. - **Don Ward**

Perception is everything

- ASK: 'What if this or that goes wrong, I look or say something stupid - drains your confidence
- A mindset of losing usually guarantees failure

Shift from right to wrong

- Instead of focusing on potential failure (What If...Down!), focus on potential success (What If...UP!)
- What if: Everything goes right, this is the best ever, I blow them away?

Make a list

- Mental or physical

Get emotional

- FEEL excited about your potential success!

Use your body

- Clench your fists and show it on your face
- Nod your head

IMPLEMENTATION

When I...

- Enter a situation that has a significant outcome and/or requires a boost of confidence

Then I will...

- Practice what if...up!

CHALLENGE: For the next 7-30 days, I challenge myself to:

- Practice what if...up before entering any social situation, and doing it with feeling/emotion!

VISUALIZE - MENTALLY REHEARSE

KEY IDEA:
Experience winning, in advance

DISCUSSION

Visualization is a powerful tool

- Visualizing lays down, in advance, the neural network needed for taking action
- Visualizing helps you see an eliminate obstacles
- A path and lack of obstacles = confidence

Winning in advance

- You have a choice of how to use this power
- People often use it wrong - they visualize failure
- See yourself winning!

How to do it

- Before entering a situation:
    - Visualize the basic action steps you will take
    - Visualize the experience of a successful outcome
    - See it, feel it, and believe it!

IMPLEMENTATION

When I...

- Enter a situation [identify a situation] that has a significant outcome and/or requires a boost of confidence

Then I will...

- Visualize - mentally rehearse a successful outcome and the steps to reach it

Made in United States
North Haven, CT
10 November 2026

22095606R00076